TRAIN TALK

TRAIN TALK

BY ROGER YEPSEN

An Illustrated Guide

to Lights, Hand Signals, Whistles,

·and Other·

Languages of Railroading

———•———

Pantheon Books

Library of Congress Cataloging in Publication Data
Yepsen, Roger B. Train talk.
Summary: An introduction to the language of railroading, in which
words, colored lights, flags, semaphore arms, coded whistles, hand signals, flares, and explosive alarms are used to guide trains and announce
their arrivals and departures.
1. Railroads—Juvenile literature.   [1. Railroads.
2. Railroads—Signaling.   3. Signals and signaling]
I. Title.   TF148.Y46   1983   625.1′65′0973   83-4062
ISBN 0-394-85750-X   ISBN 0-394-95750-4 (lib. bdg.)

To Metthea M.

CONTENTS

TRAIN TALK

STOP, LOOK, & LISTEN

One foggy night in 1920, an Indiana farmer drove home along a country road. Up ahead, a Pennsylvania Railroad train roared over a crossing. The farmer stopped and waited for the train to pass. When the last car had gone, he drove up to the tracks—and into the path of a second train that had been hidden behind the first.

So died my great-grandfather Adam, and I think of him whenever I go train watching, which is nearly every day.

You might imagine that a machine as enormous and loud as a train would be pretty hard to miss. But in spite of its air horns and bells and lights, a train ghosting down a hill can approach you as quietly as a cat. And a lone boxcar, set in motion by a switch engine at the end of a freight yard, may pick its way toward you silently, unannounced by any warning or even the sound of an engine.

Remember that an engineer doesn't have a steering wheel and can't swerve to avoid things or people in the way. That's why a locomotive has a massive snowplow or cowcatcher on the front end; if there's a snow drift or cow on the track, the train will send it flying out of the way.

Remember, too, that because trains are heavy and ride on smooth metal wheels, they can't stop very quickly.

Railroading is heavy industry, and railroads are not playgrounds. To enjoy them safely, you can either buy a ticket and go for a ride or observe the tracks from a respectful distance. Never assume that a weedy, rusty relic of a track can be used as a bench or hiking trail. A huge freight could blast around the bend at any moment, night or day, weekday or holiday—and that should be an unexpected pleasure, not a source of danger to your life and limbs.

TRAIN TALK

C H A P T E R   O N E

When you walk down to the railroad tracks, you find yourself entering another country. It's a scruffy place that hasn't changed much in a hundred years. You are likely to see old brick buildings colored faded rose and chocolate; you may notice the piney smell of creosote and the summery smell of weeds; and you'll find this a quiet place, invaded only every once in a while by the slam-bang of a passing train.

The railroad is a country that stretches from Atlantic to Pacific, from Central American jungle to Canadian tundra. Chances are, its weedy borders reach right into the heart of your own town. This country has its own land and its own telephone lines. And the railroad has its own police force because it is such a huge territory, with countless buildings and freight cars full of valuable cargo, spread along enough track in the United States alone to reach to the moon and halfway back. (These police, known to those who try to avoid them as "bulls," remove uninvited visitors from large railroad yards. In the 1920s and 1930s they rode atop boxcars with long sticks and rapped the fingers of hoboes who tried to climb aboard for a free ride.)

The railroad even has named many towns that sprang up along the tracks. Typical railroad names are Summit, Tunnelton, and anything with Junction or Station tacked on at the end. Topton, Pennsylvania, sits at the top of a long uphill climb. The Canadian Pacific Railway, faced with the task of coming up with names for new settlements along a track in Saskatchewan, simply invented an alphabetical list, from Archive through Expanse. Topping this is an alphabetical Canadian National line in Ontario that runs from Alba right through Zaru, missing only towns with names beginning with i, n, and x. On Illinois Central lines out of Decatur, Illinois, many new railroad towns borrowed names from older towns in Georgia, including Macon, Atlanta, Oconee, Ramsey, Vera, Dunn, Olney, Calhoun, Morton, Tabor, Tazewell, and Decatur itself. The area is known as Little Georgia.

There is a curious story of two railroad men who argued so long and heatedly over the best name for a little

Virginia rail town that they finally ended their dispute by inventing a brand-new name—Disputanta. And one British Columbia town that grew up along the Canadian National actually named itself Chu Chua!

Just like a country, the railroad decides how its traffic shall be run—how fast, and by what rules. On most American lines with two tracks, trains keep to the right as we do in our cars, although engineers sit on the right. Long ago, one large midwestern line began running on the left, and it still does. No government agency has interfered to tell it not to.

Traffic rules are especially important where trains must travel both ways on a single track. Two trains that meet on the same track are like two elephants that meet on a narrow path; one must pull aside to let the other pass. This is done by ducking into a siding. Which trains duck and which are free to continue on their way? A railroad may rule, for example, that northbound and eastbound trains have priority over those traveling south and west, that passenger trains should pass freights, and that long-distance freights with schedules to keep shouldn't be held up by poky local freights.

Occasionally a rule is broken, as in this example from several decades ago, when steam engines belched huge clouds of wood or coal smoke. Before pulling obediently into a siding to avoid a superior train, the crew of the humble local freight might first scan the horizon for a telltale plume of smoke. If none was spotted, the crew would try to "smoke out" the oncoming train by making it to the next siding down the line.

Railroads set their own speed limits, and these may be as low as 10 miles per hour or as high as 80, 90, or even 120. Without the government-imposed limits that control highway traffic, railroads have been free to make record-breaking runs. As early as 1893, a quite ordinary New York Central passenger train opened its throttle and ran a mile in just 32 seconds, for an amazing average speed of 112.5 miles per hour. The passengers, accustomed to walking at 3 miles per hour or cantering on a horse at 10, must have been astounded to see the landscape tearing past their windows.

The railroad not only makes its own rules but also, like most countries, has its own languages as well. These are languages of words, colored lights and flags, saluting semaphore arms, coded whistles, hand signals, flares, and explosive alarms.

How did these peculiar languages come about? Remember that the railroad is ancient by North American standards, and it has held on to many of its century-old ways. These ways seem to work well enough for all their age: just like the steam trains of the 1800s, today's metal-wheeled trains roll along metal tracks. Some passenger coaches in use today were built in the 1910s and 1920s, and a great number of stations were already old when Henry Ford sold his first car. No wonder the railroad is a country that seems to be from another time.

Meanwhile, life on both sides of the tracks has changed drastically. The train has been around long enough to see many other vehicles come and go—horse and buggy, canal barge, trolley, dirigible, and all but a few ferry boats and ocean liners. Will the automobile and truck be the next to go?

This book is a guide to the languages of railroading. Once you learn the railroad's signs and symbols, even the weediest and wobbliest of tracks will hum with excitement for you.

TRACKSIDE: SIGNALS & SIGNS

C H A P T E R   T W O

Have you noticed that trains never seem to be hijacked? That's probably because a hijacker wouldn't get very far, commandeering a vehicle without a steering wheel. The people on board a train can control only its speed and whether it travels forward or backward. For all its size and brute strength, the train goes docilely wherever it is directed by people who throw switches or push buttons along the tracks.

You'll find these men and women working in towers. *Tower* is a railroad term for a building that contains equipment for monitoring and controlling the progress of trains. If you think of a railroad system as being like a person's body, then the tower might be its brain—

but this "brain" is pretty humble compared to a sophisticated airport control tower. And if you imagine a railroad tower to be as impressive and romantic as a castle tower, you're in for a disappointment. Some older railroad towers are handsome two-story structures, but many are just little shacks with tar-paper walls, coal stoves, and outhouses tucked away in the weeds.

This chapter opens with a picture of an old wooden tower, the kind found across the continent in villages and cities, fields and forests. It guards the intersection of two rail lines. The railroad doesn't shut down at night, so there must be someone on duty at the tower around the clock, three shifts a day, every day of the year.

Upstairs in the tower is a big metal map the size of a table top, studded with lights of various colors. White lights show the progress of trains toward and away from the tower. Other lights show what the signals say out on the line and how the switches are set. Without leaving the armchair, the operator can electrically change a signal or switch a train from one track to another. It's a comfortable chair, fortunately, because the operator doesn't get to leave it often during an eight-hour vigil. This must be one of the loneliest of jobs, especially at night on a seldom traveled piece of track. Some towers are located at the ends of long dirt roads, miles from the nearest towns.

The job does bring some excitement, though. Railroad signals and switches have an important function: they keep trains from running into each other. This is crucial,

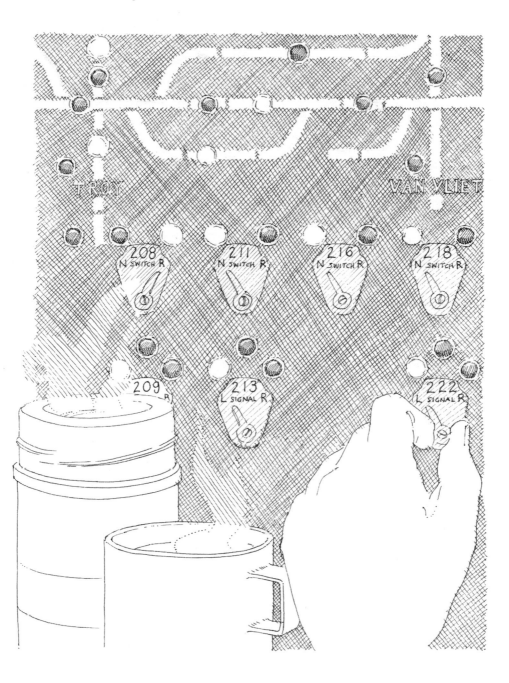

because the train is unique among vehicles in being unable to steer out of trouble. The wheels follow wherever the rails lead. A heavy train can't even stop very well because of its immense weight and the lack of traction between steel wheels and steel rails. A long freight may roll on for a mile or more after the engineer has slammed on the brakes, even with all-out emergency braking on each of the train's thousand-odd wheels.

Adding to the train's capacity for danger and destruction is the fact that at any time it may be sharing tracks with a train closing in from the opposite direction at 70 miles per hour. Single-track lines carry two-way traffic; and trains may run against the current of traffic even on lines with more than one track.

Occasionally, signals don't do their job, either because they break down or because the train crew don't notice them. When this happens, the engine crew of a hopelessly collision-bound freight may give a series of short blasts on the whistle, set the brakes, and jump out the door—a drastic act, but one that has saved many a railroader's life over the years.

Obviously, railroads seriously need the protection of signaling. They use complex systems of colored lights and the movable arms known as semaphores that are capable of giving engineers a couple of dozen messages (called indications) in addition to just "stop" and "caution" and "go."

If you watch a railroad signal for a time, you might conclude that it has a mind of its own. The signal may

appear to turn itself on and off, or decide to ripen from green to amber to ruby red. But it changes for good reason, triggered either by trains as they roll over the rails or by our lonely tower operator.

Some signals govern stretches of open track, while others control traffic across rail intersections, called interlockings. The train watcher who understands a rail line's signals can learn to tell when the next train will be along, and even from what direction. But the language of these signals changes slightly from one railroad company to another. The book that explains them all has yet to be written, and probably never will be. Each railroad has its own dialect, and the only ways to learn the quirks of your local line are to look and listen carefully, talk to railroaders, and buy an employee rule book for that particular railroad (these are occasionally sold at antique stores and used-book shops, and through ads in railroad fan magazines).

Back in the 1800s, signals were given simply by hoisting colored balls up a pole and by displaying wooden flags. The oil lamps of the time weren't bright enough to give a signal that could be seen by day. Later, lenses were developed that could beam a weak light straight ahead at the cab of an approaching engine. In fact, modern signal lights have focusing aids so that they can be aimed accurately when installed. You can see for yourself how a dim signal suddenly flares up as you walk into its intended path. With such a lens, a signal light needs very little electricity—as little as five watts, while a bedroom nightlight generally needs seven.

Old-fashioned highball signal

Curiously, it wasn't until the early 1900s that a green light came to mean that the tracks ahead were all clear. A white light was originally the "clear" signal. Red meant "stop," and either orange or green was used to indicate "caution." A couple of problems soon became obvious: a white light from a nearby house could be mistaken for the "clear" signal; so could a red signal from which the lens had fallen. Today, the use of white lights for signaling on principal tracks (called main lines) is prohibited by law in the United States.

A signal may be made up of two or three lights (or semaphore arms) on a single pole. This is done to expand the number of messages the signal can give. For example, a two- or three-part signal can give many indications that are variations on "proceed with caution," allowing trains to pass but only so far or so fast. Why bother with so many signals? The answer is that a railroad hates to bring any train to a dead stop. Time is lost, making passengers late and delaying the delivery of freight. Fuel is lost, too: depending on the current price of diesel oil, it may cost hundreds of dollars to stop a long freight and then get it back up to speed.

To make the confusing science of railroad signaling a little easier to understand, keep in mind that any signal you're apt to see operates by one of the four basic methods shown on the following pages: color-light signals, position-light signals, color-position signals, and semaphores.

COLOR-LIGHT SIGNALS are something like highway traffic lights. The familiar red, yellow, and green lights may be arranged in a triangle, horizontal row, or vertical row (usually with green on top, in what's called an Irish arrangement of the three colors). Or there may be just one light, as illustrated here. This is known as a searchlight or bull's-eye signal; behind its clear lens, colored lenses can shift into position to give the three colors.

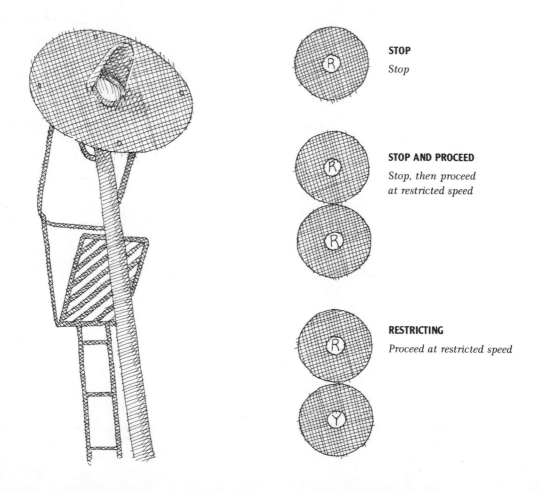

STOP

Stop

STOP AND PROCEED

Stop, then proceed at restricted speed

RESTRICTING

Proceed at restricted speed

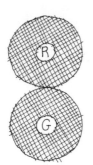

MEDIUM CLEAR

Proceed at medium speed

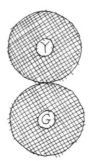

APPROACH MEDIUM

*Proceed, approaching
next signal at
medium speed*

APPROACH

*Proceed, preparing
to stop at
next signal*

or

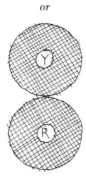

CLEAR

Proceed

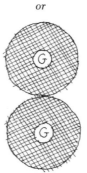

or

COLOR-LIGHT ARRANGEMENTS

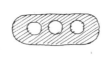

R = red

Y = yellow

G = green

POSITION-LIGHT SIGNALS are found on the former Pennsylvania, Lehigh Valley, and Long Island railroads (now parts of Conrail). The lights are grouped in vertical, diagonal, and horizontal rows on a large black metal disc or discs. All the lights are the same color, a pale yellow that is especially easy to see through fog. The indication being given is determined by which row is illuminated. Most signals have three rows of lights, but some have four, others just two. A pale yellow light on the signal mast is used to give a greater variety of messages.

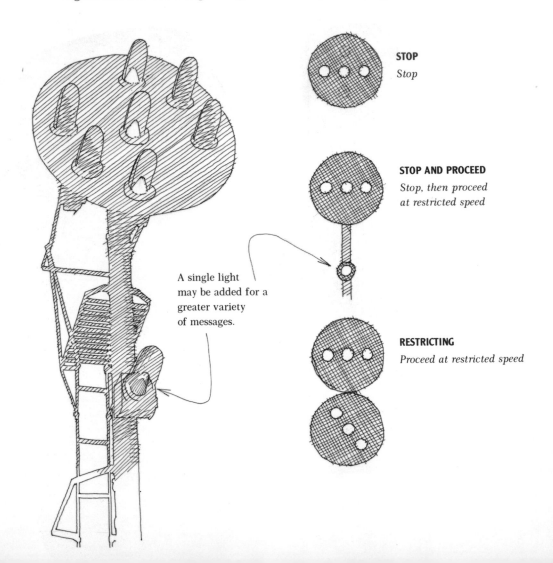

STOP
Stop

STOP AND PROCEED
Stop, then proceed at restricted speed

A single light may be added for a greater variety of messages.

RESTRICTING
Proceed at restricted speed

PERMISSIVE

*Track ahead occupied;
proceed, prepared to
stop short of train*

APPROACH MEDIUM

*Proceed, approaching
next signal at
medium speed*

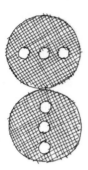

MEDIUM CLEAR

Proceed at medium speed

CLEAR

Proceed

APPROACH

*Proceed, preparing
to stop at
next signal*

SPECIAL INDICATIONS

Go into the siding ahead

*Lower the pantograph
(an extendable arm on
top of an electric train
that picks up current
from overhead wires)*

All lights shown here are pale yellow.

The **COLOR-POSITION SIGNALS** used by the Baltimore & Ohio look something like position-light signals. But there are only two lights in a row, not three, and these lights give indications both by position and by color—red, yellow, green, and a peculiar bluish shade called lunar white. In addition, white lights are placed above and below the cluster of colored lights for a greater variety of messages.

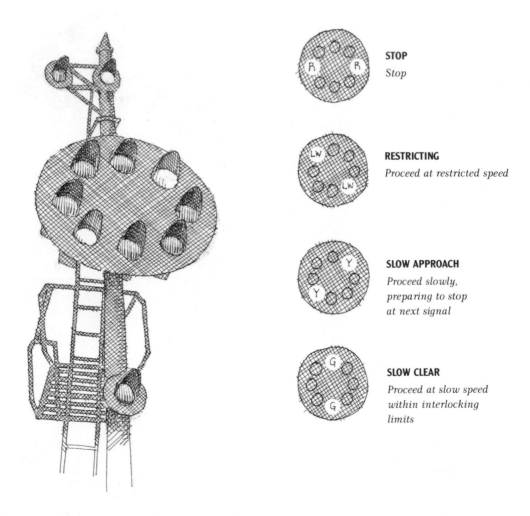

STOP
Stop

RESTRICTING
Proceed at restricted speed

SLOW APPROACH
Proceed slowly, preparing to stop at next signal

SLOW CLEAR
Proceed at slow speed within interlocking limits

MEDIUM CLEAR
Proceed at medium speed

APPROACH
*Proceed, preparing
to stop at
next signal*

APPROACH MEDIUM
*Proceed, approaching
next signal at
medium speed*

CLEAR
Proceed

R = red

LW = lunar white

Y = yellow

G = green

W = white

SEMAPHORES, once the most common of signals, are seen only on certain lines today. (They're still a favorite on model train layouts, however.) The semaphore gives the indication by the angle of a moving arm of wood or metal—vertical, diagonal, or horizontal—and also by moving a green, yellow, or red lens in front of a fixed white light, so that the signal can be read at night as well. Even the shape of the arm's tip means something to the railroader.

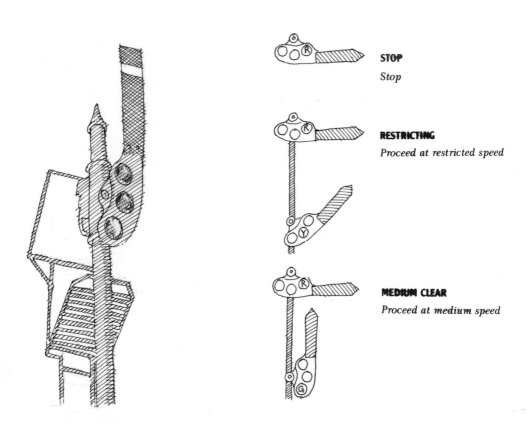

STOP

Stop

RESTRICTING

Proceed at restricted speed

MEDIUM CLEAR

Proceed at medium speed

APPROACH

*Proceed, preparing
to stop at
next signal*

CLEAR

Proceed

or

or

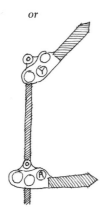

APPROACH MEDIUM

*Proceed, approaching
next signal at
medium speed*

R = red

Y = ycllow

G = green

BLADE TYPES

Distant   *Home*   *Block*   *Train order*

☞ Dwarf Signals

Each style of signal—color-light, position-light, color-position, and semaphore—has its own type of dwarf signal. These small, ground-hugging signals aren't meant to be read by foot-high engineers. They give orders to slower trains, those leaving a siding for the main line or backing up or traveling through yards. In the yards of some railroads, purple lenses are used instead of red on dwarf signals, to avoid distracting engineers of nearby main-line trains who are on the alert for red signals. The drawing shows a position-light dwarf signal.

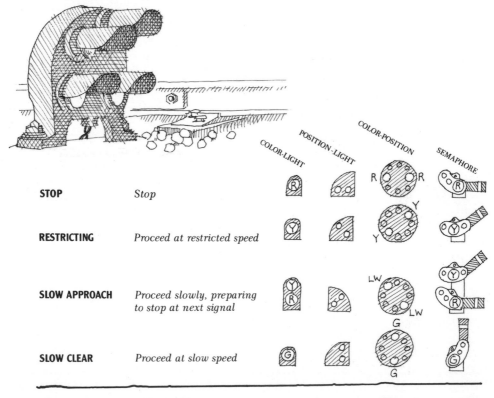

		COLOR-LIGHT	POSITION-LIGHT	COLOR-POSITION	SEMAPHORE
STOP	*Stop*	R		R — R	R
RESTRICTING	*Proceed at restricted speed*	Y		Y	Y
SLOW APPROACH	*Proceed slowly, preparing to stop at next signal*	Y R		LW — LW	Y R
SLOW CLEAR	*Proceed at slow speed*	G		G — G	G

| **R** = red | **Y** = yellow | **G** = green | **LW** = lunar white |

Signaling Systems ✑

A rounded-tip semaphore is used on one of the simplest and oldest of signaling systems, known as a *train-order operation*. It works today much as it did way back before the Civil War. Semaphores are placed at stations along the line. The station agent operates the signal, not to tell train crews to stop or go but to let them know whether or not they are supposed to pick up written instructions, known as train orders (or flimsies, because the paper is thin to allow for making legible carbon copies). A green signal (with the semaphore arm straight up) means there are no orders to be picked up and the train can continue on its way. A yellow light (with the arm at a 45-degree angle) tells the crew to pick up written orders "on the fly." That is, the operator or station agent holds the order at the end of a long stick, known as an order stick or hoop, so that the piece of paper can be grabbed by the engineer as the train rolls by. Often a second copy is offered to the conductor back in the caboose. The sticks are usually Y-shaped, the fork holding a triangular loop of string onto which the rolled-up order has been tied. Orders may be handed up from the ground or out of a tower window. A red light (with the arm horizontal) usually commands the crew to stop to pick up orders and sign for them.

Instead of a semaphore, the order signal may be a colored hand lantern or even just a painted wooden panel called an order board. This is old-fashioned railroading,

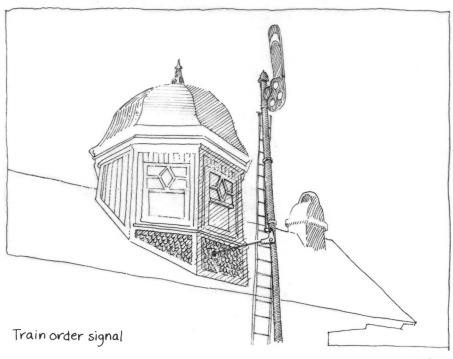

Train order signal

Order board

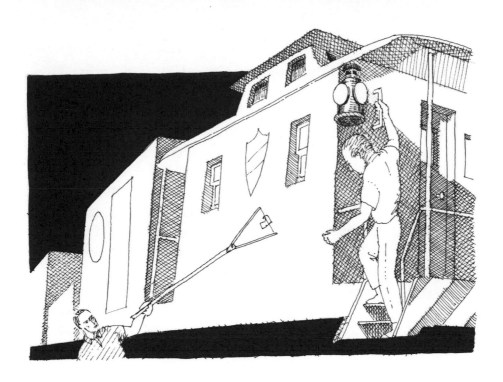

and a line that is controlled by train orders sometimes goes by the quaint term *dark territory*.

More advanced is the *manual block system*. With this system, tower operators tell trains whether or not they can enter the next stretch of track, or block, and at what speed. Normally, only one train can be in a block at a time. The operator changes a block signal to read "stop" as a train passes, and does not return it to read "approach" ("caution") or "clear" until informed by phone (telegraph, in years past) that the train has just passed the next operator down the line. This manual system takes a lot of employees, stationed every five to fifteen miles or so, all day and often through the night. That means a big payroll for the railroad and also allows plenty of chances for human error. For these reasons, railroads are gradually changing to *automated block systems,* with block signals that are triggered electrically by the passage of the trains themselves. On such lines, abandoned block towers are a common sight, with their windows boarded up and their electrical guts having been ripped out and used for scrap. A single dispatcher at a centralized control station may be responsible for hundreds of miles of tracks.

A train trips the electrical signal as it travels. The rails carry a weak electrical current, and when trackside monitors detect that a train's steel wheels and axles have created a short circuit between rails, the signal is set to read "stop." The signal remains in this indication until the train has left the electrical circuit of the block.

Each block is electrically isolated from its neighboring blocks with insulated rail joints. You can see thin strips of nonconductive material between the last rails of one block and the first of the next block. The rail ends may also be insulated with paint.

Depending on their complexity, block signals can indicate whether the coast is clear, not just in the next block but perhaps in the two or three after that. In effect, this allows the engineer to see far into the distance, around mountains and through tunnels. And this in turn allows railroads to run their trains faster and closer together without sacrificing safety.

So much for block signals. They are pretty hard to understand until you actually go outside and watch them for a while. The second way signals are used is more familiar, and something like a highway traffic light. These *interlocking signals* guard an interlocking, an intersection of tracks, making certain that only one of the intersecting lines is given permission to proceed at any one time. The signal to the other route says "stop" in no uncertain terms. Interlocking signals come in pairs—a home signal at the intersection, and a distant signal placed a few thousand feet down the tracks to warn train crews that the all-important home signal is about to ap-

Home signal

Distant signal

pear. The upper light of a distant signal is placed a bit to the right of the lower one so that it won't be confused with the vertical arrangement of lights on a home signal. Also, the arms of semaphore distant signals may have a notched fishtail shape to set them apart from the squared-off arms that are the mark of interlocking signals (and the pointed arms of block signals).

Interlockings may be protected by other systems thought up by individual railroads—as simple as a gate that swings to block one line or the other, or as ingenious as this curious method used at an interlocking in Camilla, Georgia. A train crew can get a clear signal to cross the interlocking only when a trainman leaves the train, goes into an unoccupied building near the tracks, and throws a lever. When that lever is thrown, not only does the semaphore move to read "clear," but the building's door also locks automatically. Only after the train has passed the interlocking and the crew member has restored the signal to its stop position can he or she leave to rejoin the train.

☞ Switch Signals

Switches control the direction a train will take. A switch is used wherever a sidetrack departs from the main track, such as at an industry siding or a branch line. The switch is little more than two movable rails at the very end of that sidetrack. If the train is to leave the main line for this track, the switch rails (also called points) are shifted to catch the rims (flanges) of the cars' steel wheels; if the train is to continue straight ahead, the switch points are kept several inches from the main-line rails. The switch points may be shifted (thrown) either by a hand-operated metal arm at trackside or by a machine that is operated remotely from a tower.

The crew of a train are greatly interested in knowing which way a switch is set. If they are traveling down the main line at a high speed and come upon a switch that is mistakenly set for a siding, their train may be sent flying off the track. Most turns must be entered slowly. Switches are kept locked because a switch that is tampered with could cause a serious derailment.

The crew can see how a switch is set by the position of either a lantern with four colored lenses or brightly colored metal targets. These pivot when the switch is thrown. A switch set safely for continuing straight ahead will display green lights (or targets) to the main line, and red to the sidetrack. If the crew of a main-line train see a red light or target, they know their train will be diverted to the sidetrack. Different colors may be used on less important lines and in yards—yellow for "straight ahead," and blue or purple to indicate that a switch has been thrown to another track. At night, a yard equipped with dim, colored switch lights looks something like a harbor with its distant buoy lights.

The old-fashioned kerosene switch lantern is fast disappearing from the railroad in favor of electric models or metal flags with round reflectors like the kind used on the back of a bicycle. A kerosene lantern is troublesome because it must be refilled with fuel periodically and its wick must be adjusted. Many old lanterns have been electrified; others have been sold off and are now collectors' items.

☞ *Other Signals and Signs*

The "whistle" sign is a common feature of the railroad landscape. It is placed before highway crossings, bridges, and tunnels—wherever the tracks might be blocked by people or cars or animals. It tells the engineer to sound the most common of whistle messages—two long blasts, one short, and another long. The sign usually bears a big *W* for "whistle," painted on or stamped out of or cast into metal, but whistles went out with the steam engine a few decades ago, to be replaced by air horns. Air horns are probably just as loud, and on some engines the horns play an attractive chord, but the steam whistle had a special, eerie, animal-like shriek that, once heard, was not soon forgotten.

In snow country, look for the "flanger" sign. It takes all sorts of forms, but its purpose is the same on any railroad—to warn snow-plow crews that their plow (or flanger) may be snagged by an obstruction just ahead. The sign posts may be old boiler tubes, recycled from the innards of steam engines.

Nowadays, all signals work by sight and sound. But there used to be one that worked by touch. You may have seen a row of weighted ropes dangling above the tracks. These "telltales" (also known as rattails) were intended to warn brakemen atop boxcars that they were approaching a low bridge or tunnel and that they'd better duck. When a brakeman felt the brush of the ropes, there was just time enough to hit the deck. Telltales don't serve any purpose today. Back before air-powered brakes were placed at the engineer's fingertips, a brakeman climbed on top of a car to set the brakes by hand.

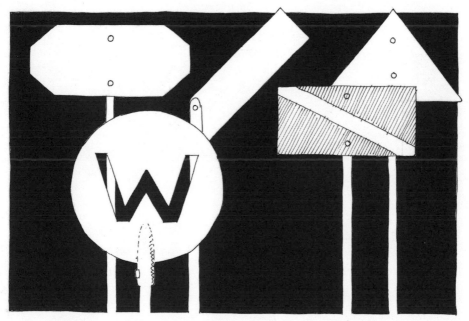

Four flanger signs and a whistle sign with a cutout W.

This was done by means of a big wheel on each car, and so the brakeman had to rush from car to car as the train rolled down a hill. Now the brakeman sits snugly in the caboose or engine, and the telltales just swing in the wind.

Look down a sidetrack, past the switch lantern or flag, and you may see another lantern or flag set quite close to the ground. This signal indicates whether or not the sidetrack is blocked by a curious safety device known as a derail. The derail spares a lot of trouble by causing a little trouble: that is, this block of metal perches atop a rail and directs runaway cars off the track before they can drift out onto the main line and cause a big wreck. The idea is, of course, that it's better to have one or two wheels of a freight car go off the track than to allow the car to get in the way of high-speed trains on the main line.

When the crew of a sidetracked train want to enter the main line, they throw the switch in their direction and the derail automatically slides from the rail. That's because the switch and derail are connected by a long pipe that shifts back and forth on rollers. The derail lantern is tied in so that it turns to show the sidetrack is clear when the derail moves out of the train's way.

Everyone is familiar with the large white X and flashing red lights at railroad crossings that warn drivers of cars and trucks that a train is coming. These so-called crossbucks, along with automatic crossing gates, have

nearly done away with an old, old occupation—that of the crossing watchman. This person spends the day in a tiny building heated by a coal stove and equipped with a bell. When the bell rings, that means a train is on its way. The watchman picks up a flag or stop sign, leaves the shack, and stands by the crossing to keep cars, trucks, and daring pedestrians from trying to beat the train.

Sometimes the tiny buildings were placed on tall towers to give the watchman the best possible view of the tracks. These elevated towers are something of a rarity these days. From them, little levers may be flicked to turn stoplights red or lower crossing gates and control traffic in the streets below as a train approaches.

Train watching doesn't always mean hanging around well-worn railroads in an ancient part of town, of course. Among the most fascinating rail signals are the white lights embedded in the station platforms of the recently built Metro mass-transit system in and around Washington, D.C. These signals are for the information of passengers about to board trains, not for employees. When no train is around, they glow dimly, as if sulking. People awaiting a train know one is drawing near when the lights brighten. The lights begin to pulse dramatically just before the train pulls in. They are at their brightest when the train is in the station, and then they ebb gradually to let late-arriving people know they've just missed a train.

ON BOARD: LIGHTS, HORNS, FLAGS, & SMALL EXPLOSIONS

C H A P T E R   T H R E E

Because a train is a huge object that can't steer out of danger, its crew go to a lot of trouble to let the world know the train is coming.

Lights

An engine crew use lights and sounds to warn grade-crossing traffic, other trains, and people and animals near the tracks. Headlights are kept on at all times, with one exception: on a single-track line, a train that has pulled safely into a siding must extinguish its headlight so that the crew of an oncoming train won't panic at seeing what appears to be another train on their track.

The front of the engine carries other lights as well. Some railroads install a revolving bubble light, like the kind used on police cars, which is kept on all the time. On the Seaboard Coast Line, a strobe light is activated when the engineer blows the air horn. Another attention-getting device is the Mars light, a headlight that wobbles about behind its lens to produce a very eerie effect.

Small lights called classification lights can be seen on either side of the engine's headlights. They are weaker than headlights and look something like automobile turn signals. But classification lights don't signal by blinking; their messages are color-coded. The colors are changed from within the engine. By day, colored flags may be used instead.

An engine displaying red lights or flags is really at the back of the train, pushing instead of pulling. The lights serve as taillights; they also let railroaders know which end of the train is which—no small matter if a train has engines on both ends. Commuter trains often run this way so that the engine doesn't have to be switched from one end of the train to the other after each short trip. And a heavy freight train may have an extra engine placed on the back end for a push up steep mountain grades.

Two green lights or flags warn that the train will be

followed by a train called a section, needed to carry an overflow of passengers or freight cars that couldn't be accommodated by the first. (One night the New York Central's sleeping-car-only *Twentieth Century Limited* ran in a record total of seven sections to accommodate all the people who wanted to buy tickets.)

Two white classification lights or flags mark the locomotive of a so-called extra train, one not listed in the timetables but run because of special need. Extras include work trains for track crews, inspection trains for railroad officials, and passenger trains run for special events, such as ski trips and political campaign tours.

If there is no special message to give, as is usually the case, the engine will display neither flags nor classification lights.

Traditionally, the rear of a train carries two colored lights called markers. Some trains simply display a single red flag or blinking red light at the tail end, but the standard marker light has four lenses, one red and three amber. Usually, amber shows to the sides and red to the rear. If the train is waiting on a siding, both lights are turned to show amber to the rear, as assurance to a train coming from behind that the waiting train isn't sitting in its way.

Occasionally, you'll see a stopped car or train with a blue flag or lantern on it. This signal warns that the car or train is not to be moved, for the safety of people who might be working on it. For example, when an Amtrak train changes from electric engines to diesels, as happens at the ends of its electrified track in Connecticut, Pennsylvania, southern New York State, and Washington, D.C., a blue lantern is hung on the engine until the station employees have disconnected it from the train—a potentially hazardous job that requires them to walk between the engine and first car.

☞ Horns

The air horns of a diesel locomotive are as loud as fire sirens, and for a good reason. Once under way, a twenty-million-pound freight won't stop for anything or anyone in its immediate path. It can't—the heavier a vehicle is, the more effort is needed to stop it, and the freight train is the heaviest of land vehicles.

If you've ever heard a train's horn, it was probably giving the standard warning at a highway crossing. But the air horns are used for more than scaring the daylights out of people and animals. The engineer can blast signals to the crew inside the train or on the ground. One message tells the flagman of a train making an unscheduled stop to walk back down the tracks and stop oncoming trains. Other codes warn the rear-end crew that the engineer is about to either release or apply the brakes. Some codes are common, and others, quite rare. Most are heard less frequently now that the railroad uses radio communication, including hand-held walkie-talkies.

On passenger trains, members of the crew can hike up through the train to the locomotive if they have something to report to the engineer. But rather than make this long, bouncy journey, they can send a message via a special air line (or an electric line on newer equipment) that runs through the cars and ends with a small whistle (or buzzer) in the locomotive cab. Messages are sent by means of a valve in each car. Shown on page 46 are the standard signals sent from train to locomotive cab.

Such signal lines don't exist on freight trains, and so a freight's crew back in the caboose must use either radios

---

ENGINE WHISTLE SIGNALS

O	Apply brakes. Stop.
— —	Release brakes. Proceed.
— O O O	Flagman protect rear of train.
— — — —	(Single or two main tracks): Flagman may return from south or west.
— — — — —	Flagman may return from north or east.
O O O	When standing, back up.
O O O O	Call for signals.
— — — —	Approaching junctions, railroad crossings at grade, stations.
O —	Inspect train line for leak or for brakes sticking.
SERIES OF SHORT SOUNDS	To warn persons or animals on tracks.

O = A SHORT BLAST ON THE LOCOMOTIVE'S WHISTLE
— = A LONG BLAST

TRAIN LINE SIGNALS

O O
   When standing, start.
   When running, stop at once.

O O O
   When standing, back up.
   When running, stop at next passenger station.

O O O O
   When standing, apply or release brakes.
   When running, reduce speed.

O O O O O
   When standing, recall flagman.
   When running, increase speed.

O O O O O O
   When running, increase train heat.

O — — O
   Shut off train heat.

— — — —
   When running, brakes sticking;
   look back for hand signals.

or hand signals, with lanterns by night, to communicate with the front end.

☞ *Hand Signals*

You can't just yell at a moving train and expect the engineer to understand you. A train is just too big and too noisy. That's why railroad people developed hand signals for telling the engineer to stop or go or slow down. The hand signals shown here have been in use for more than a hundred years, and they are as much a part of the railroader's language as the words *stop* and *go*.

To make these signals easier to see, a red flag (or a handkerchief at least) is often used by day, and a white lantern at night. On the railroad, the hand lantern is the basic signaling tool. Lanterns were once almost invariably lit by kerosene, but now most are battery-powered. Lanterns come with glass globes that can be clear, green, blue, and red. Often a metal part is stamped with the name or initials of the railroad; occasionally the glass globe is embossed with the railroad's symbol (the Baltimore & Ohio featured its symbol, the Capitol dome, on its lantern globes). These lanterns are made for heavy use, with galvanized coating and a wire cage protecting the globe.

Not all hand signals tell trains to stop and go. Some

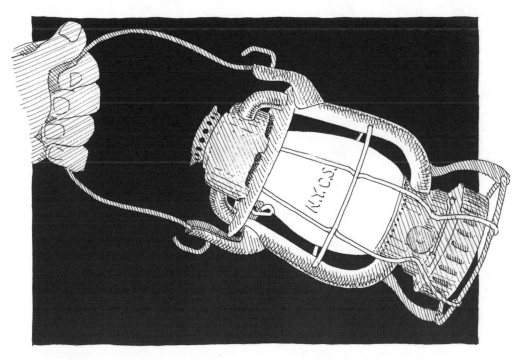

Stop

Reduce speed

Apply brakes

Release brakes

Back up

Proceed

warn train crews of dangers, and others are just friendly greetings. One signal has the important function of warning a train crew that a wheel bearing is producing smoke or flames, a condition known as a hotbox. But it is a funny signal to give: one hand points to the wheel of the train, and the other holds the nose. At night, the same message is given by swinging a lantern vertically in a small circle, with the lantern held by the wire cage.

If the brakes are sticking and smoking, a railroader alerts the crew by shoving both hands away from the body in a sliding motion; at night, a lantern is shoved away from the body. Another signal is used by a hungry member of a train crew as mealtime approaches. One hand is held below the mouth and the other shovels in imaginary food. The message is "Let's eat!" If the signaler has an obviously worried expression, the signal means "Can we eat?"

Two or more signals can be strung together to make a sentence, such as "Stop the train clear of the main line, uncouple the last car, and we'll go eat."

Railroaders watch passing trains to see that all is in order. If they see nothing wrong, they give the caboose crew the "proceed" signal (also known as a highball) by pulling an imaginary whistle cord over the head up and down several times. But in the event of serious trouble, they follow Rule 12-h from the employee rulebook: "Any object waved violently by anyone on or near the tracks is a signal to stop." Anyone includes you, and obviously this warning is not to be given except in an emergency.

It is, however, perfectly all right to greet a train by giving the highball sign. If the engineer is in a good mood and not busy, you might get a couple of toots in return.

☞ *Fusees and Torpedoes*

When a train breaks down or can't keep up speed because of bad weather or mechanical problems, it can't just pull off the road and let traffic go by. Instead, it must stay on the tracks, where it is a sitting duck. Unless the line is controlled by automatic block signals, the crew must protect the train from the possibility of collision by warning oncoming traffic.

If the train is moving slowly and behind schedule, red flares can be thrown down to the tracks as a warning to following trains, which otherwise would expect it to be long gone. These flares are called fusees. They are a part of every train's emergency equipment. (If you see one burning on the tracks, do not remove it.)

If the train comes to a dead stop, the flagman is ready for an order from the engineer to protect the train. When that message comes, by whistle or radio, the unlucky flagman hikes back down the tracks carrying a lantern (or flag by day), fusees, and large explosive caps known as torpedoes. (On a single-track line, a head-end trainman may hike *up* the tracks to warn trains approaching from that direction, too.)

This is a lousy job on a cold, blustery night, and over the years many lives have been lost because the railroader didn't hike quite far enough to stop an oncoming train in time. How far is far enough? An old rule of thumb is "A dime will get you a quarter," meaning that for every ten miles per hour of the track's speed limit, the flagman must walk back a quarter mile. On a 40-mile-per-hour line, for example, the flagman would have a mile-long hike.

Once at a distance sufficient to protect the train, the flagman places two torpedoes on the rails, securing them with metal clips. The first train to run over that spot will explode the torpedoes with a noise loud enough to warn the locomotive crew above to slow their train and proceed one mile at reduced speed.

When the trouble clears up, the engineer of the stalled train sounds four longs to call in the flagman from the south or west, and five longs to call in the person guarding the tracks to the north or east. This is a welcome sound, and the flagman hurries back to the train, perhaps giving the up-and-down highball signal while climbing back on board to let the engineer know it's okay to go. Occasionally a train has pulled away without its flagman, leaving that sorry railroader to walk to the nearest phone or wait for the next train.

☞ *Flag Stops*

Passenger trains are usually in a great hurry, and they may stop at certain smaller towns only if flagged down by a ticket agent or even by passengers who want to get on or off. These towns are called flag stops and are indicated as such in timetables.

If you're on a train and want to get off at a flag stop, that's easy enough. The conductor knows you've purchased a ticket to that point, and will warn the engineer to stop. But if you want to get *on* a train at a flag stop, and that town hasn't an agent to let the train crew know you're there, then you have to flag the train down and hope for the best. You stand well off to the side and wave your arms vigorously. But there's no guarantee the train will see you in time to stop, and so it's best to tell the railroad that you'll be standing there. The flag-stop footnote on Amtrak's timetables reads, "Where possible, please give sufficient advance notice to agent or conductor." If the flag stop has no agent, you might call the next station up or down the line.

If all goes well, the engineer will brake to a smooth stop, a door will open, and a trainman will step down to help you aboard, wiping off the handrail and placing a little footstool on the ground for your convenience. Once safely aboard, you can buy your ticket.

So it has been at hundreds of humble towns across the continent since railroads began. Being at a flag stop is better than having no trains stop at all. And it's a thrill to

bend the iron	*throw a switch*	dry hopper	*old-fashioned waterless toilet*
big hook	*wrecking crane*	joining the birds	*leaping from a train before an unavoidable accident*
boomer	*railroader who restlessly changes jobs*		
brains	*conductor*	monkey	*derail mechanism*
clear board	*green or clear signal*	nosebag	*lunch brought from home*
Cleopatra	*railroad business car*	red eye	*stop signal*
crummy	*caboose*	reefer	*refrigerated car*
deadhead	*railroader riding free, or passenger car traveling empty*	varnish	*passenger cars or train*
		window music	*passing scenery*

see a passenger stop a hurtling, million-pound object just by waving at it.

Railroad Slang ☜

A family or a group of close friends often make up their own words and phrases to describe things—terms that wouldn't mean much to someone else.

Railroaders have been inventing such terms since the 1830s and have built up a rich vocabulary. Many of the terms are needed to describe things that simply didn't exist until the railroad invented them—flag stops, locomotives, and brakemen, for example. Others serve a purpose but are also fun to say—like *hogger* ("engineer"), *dump the air* ("put on the air brakes"), *gandy dancer* ("track worker"), and *frog* (for the piece of metal where two rails cross each other, X-shaped and looking nothing like an amphibian). Some railroading terms have found their way into everyday use, such as *highball, one-track mind,* and *asleep at the switch.* If you hang around railroad people, you'll hear plenty more examples of this one-hundred-fifty-year-old language.

TIMETABLES, TICKETS, & WATCHES

C H A P T E R   F O U R

A timetable tells you where a train will go and when. The stops are listed, one after another, with the estimated time of departure for each. For big stations where the train will stay a while—to pick up and drop off cars, or change crews and engines—the timetable may also give an arrival time.

Timetables are handed out free by the railroad. Some timetables, like the one reproduced later in this chapter, just list one route. A system timetable, on the other hand, gives all the routes of a railroad. Bigger still is a book called *The Official Railway Guide* (formerly *The Official Guide of the Railways*), which prints timetables for all the long-distance passenger trains in the United States, Mexico, and Canada. Because there are far fewer passenger trains running today than in years past, the *Guide* is now slimmer than older issues, which ran over a thousand pages.

Even though no longer of practical use to the traveler, these older *Guides* are great fun to browse through and have become collector's items. Studying the thousands of trains, you can make up an imaginary trip from your town to almost any other town on the continent, via any of several trains with their various sleeping accommodations, dining cars, lounge and library cars, observation cars, and so on. The names of the trains themselves are enough to set your imagination to work: *Afternoon Hiawatha, Aztec Eagle, Choctaw Rocket, Fast Flying Virginian, Flying Crow, Iron and Copper Country Express, Land O'Corn, Mark Twain Zephyr, Night Cape Codder, Orange Blossom Special, Streamlined Meteor,* and the famous *Wabash Cannonball.*

If you enjoy reading timetables and traveling in your imagination, you might try to find an inexpensive, more recent *Guide* at antique stores and used-book stores, or perhaps through one of the several rail fan magazines available at newsstands (the best of these is *Trains*).

As an example of the travels you can take without leaving your armchair, let's plan a journey by browsing through the timetables published in a fat, yellowing copy of *The Official Guide* for 1908. We'll imagine ourselves in Cincinnati, bound for our home in Doe Run, a village south of St. Louis, Missouri. In the thousand-plus pages of timetables, we find several ways of making the trip, some more direct than others. Obvious choices for the leg to St. Louis are via the Baltimore & Ohio and the New York Central, offering five daily trains apiece. Or we can take a less-traveled route on the Vandalia Line, Illinois Central, or Louisville & Nashville connecting with the Louisville, Henderson & St. Louis. But a scrappy little line catches our attention with its boasts of "Perfect Passenger Service." This road, the Toledo, St. Louis & Western, is no longer around, but in 1908 it went by the nickname The Clover Leaf Route and promised "No Dirt, No Dust, No Smoke, No Cinders"—these having been the chief bugaboos of people traveling behind coal-burning locomotives in open-windowed cars.

We'll buy tickets on the railroad's Number 5, the *Commercial Traveler*. But to reach the train we have to grab Chicago-bound Number 31 of the Pittsburgh, Cincinnati, Chicago & St. Louis (known simply as The Pennsylvania Short Line), leaving town at 2:00 P.M. and getting us in to Kokomo, Indiana, on the Clover Leaf Route, at 7:40 that evening. That leaves us some time to stroll around Kokomo because the *Traveler* isn't due in until 14 minutes after midnight. By that hour we'll be ready for our berths in the *Traveler*'s observation sleeper. This car is placed at the rear of the train and has windows in the back for a good view of the receding landscape.

We'll arrive in St. Louis at 5:50 the next evening—

just 19 minutes after the last run for the day of the Mississippi River & Bonne Terre, the railroad that could have taken us straight home to Doe Run. Unless the *Traveler* pulls in early, that means a hotel room in St. Louis and an early start the next morning on the MR & BT's Number 21, departing at 7:30 A.M. But we thumb through the *Guide* and find that, if we still feel adventuresome at this point in our journey, we can have breakfast aboard the broiler-buffet sleeper of the St. Louis, Iron Mountain & Southern's Number 5. This train is bound for faraway places—Mexico City—but we'll get off just a few stops down the line, in Bismarck, where our train will be met by a local running to Doe

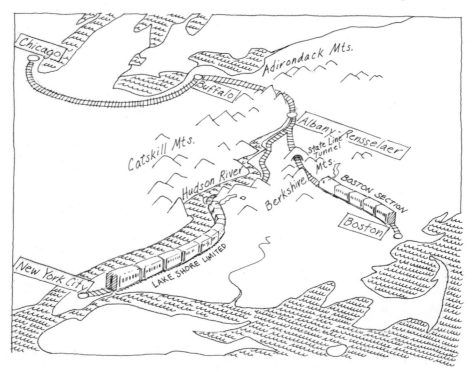

Run. We will be home at 17 minutes past noon. It has taken us almost two days to travel 478 miles.

Here is a modern-day schedule for Amtrak's *Lake Shore Limited,* an overnight train running on the route between New York City and Chicago, with a sleeping car added from a Boston section that meets the *Lake Shore* at Albany-Rensselaer, New York.

This is a daily run, which means that each evening a train leaves New York and another leaves Chicago. The *Lake Shore* is a named train, which means it has a little more personality and prestige than short commuter runs that are known simply by numbers. A railroad names those of its trains that carry the best equipment—parlor

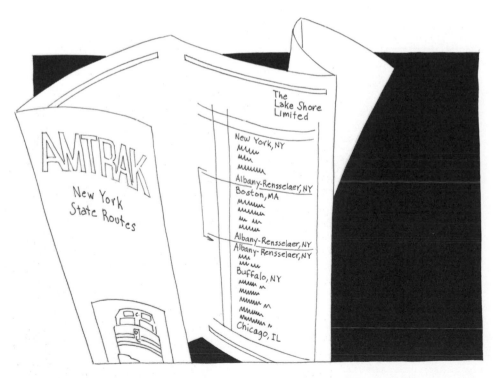

The
Lake Shore
Limited

New York, NY

Albany-Rensselaer, NY
Boston, MA

Albany-Rensselaer, NY
Albany-Rensselaer, NY

Buffalo, NY

Chicago, IL

AMTRAK

New York
State Routes

cars with big upholstered armchairs, dining cars with flowers on each table, and sleeping cars with fold-down beds. The best of the named trains have been called limiteds because they stop only at larger cities and carry only first-class passengers who may pay extra to ride in parlor and sleeping cars. Some railroads went so far as to roll out a red carpet to meet limiteds as they pulled into the station.

So it once was. No longer do the railroads of the United States and Canada run first-class trains of just sleepers and parlor cars. All trains now include coaches—cars containing rows of seats.

Timetables for long-distance trains include a list of equipment—coaches, dining cars, dome cars, and various kinds of sleepers. The list for the *Lake Shore* shows that sleeping-car service is available on the Boston-to-Albany section, and that the sleeper runs straight through to Chicago so that passengers don't have to leave their bedrooms in Albany to change trains.

☞ **Tickets**

Another piece of paper important to the railroad passenger is the ticket, or seat check. It shows you paid your money and tells how far you paid to go. It will also indicate if you paid extra for a lounge seat or a berth in a sleeping car. On your walks up and down the length of a train, the ticket is like a school kid's hall pass: you are supposed to have it with you at all times.

When the trainmen and their boss, the conductor, go through the cars checking on tickets, they may even knock on bathroom doors and ask that the occupants slip their tickets under the door for inspection. This practice led to a trick that you may have seen in old movies. A person boards a train without buying a ticket and knocks on the door of an occupied bathroom with the stern command, "Your ticket, please!" A ticket appears below the door, and the freeloading passenger takes it and walks briskly to another car.

When railroad employees punch your ticket, they are

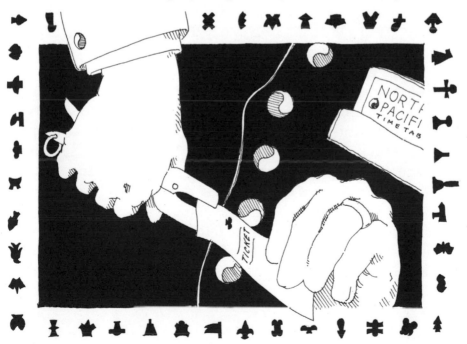

signing it with their names—not with a signature but with their own shape of punch. One punch company has advertised that it stocks more than five hundred different patterns—hearts, wavy lines, lopsided squares, and so on. In this way, each ticket carries a record of who checked it over a journey.

☞ Railroad Time

Before railroads first linked the towns across North America, each town set its clocks by the sun. In those days, the clocks of the next town to the west would be a few minutes slower than your own because the sun visited there a little later each day; the next town to the east would be running a few minutes ahead.

This casual method of timekeeping served just fine for many years. But a railroad couldn't very well run its trains on time if every station set its clocks and watches independently. So, the railroad picked one standard time and stuck to it. The towns along the line soon set their timepieces by the trains going past, and by the 1880s, the continent was divided up into the several time zones we know today.

The railroad was known for its habit of careful timekeeping. On the former Lehigh Valley Railroad, for example, standard clocks were maintained along the route.

Each morning at 9:00, a call went out to dozens of these locations, giving the exact time according to the Washington Observatory. Employees were to check their pocket watches by these clocks each day, and each month they turned their watches over to a railroad-appointed inspector for checking and cleaning. A record of these inspections, Form T 90, was handed to the railroad superintendent each April and October.

Railroads are now more relaxed about timekeeping. Though watches must still be inspected, it happens less often, and the railroad may approve of electronic wristwatches as well as the big, palm-filling mechanical pocket watches, such as the traditional 21- and 23-jewel Hamiltons that conductors and engineers once favored.

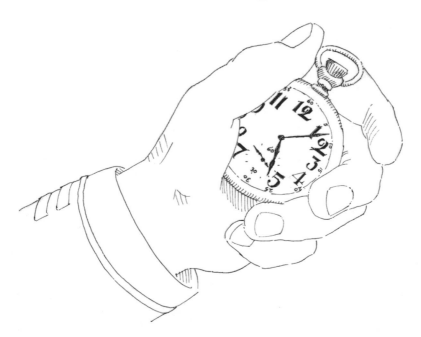

ARD
9
000
500
900

READING A BOXCAR

C H A P T E R   F I V E

At rest on a siding, a boxcar looks like part of the land-scape. In fact, there was a time when most boxcars were painted barn red and could almost be mistaken for little barns or covered bridges. Barn red was a popular color, not so much for its looks as for its cheapness: it was made of little more than rust and turpentine.

Besides carrying freight around the countryside and looking picturesque, boxcars carry a variety of messages. Most obvious is the logo—a stylish combination of let-ters or words, often simply a picture, that is a railroad company's symbol. The Norfolk & Western stenciled on its cars an unimaginative squiggle made up of the line's

initials. Most logos are more interesting. Maine Central is known by a pine tree, Canadian National by a maple leaf, Canadian Pacific by a beaver, and the Chessie System by a sleeping cat.

Some boxcars carry the railroad's nickname. Nicknames are easier to remember than the gangly official names that some lines were born with. For example, *Nickel Plate* is a lot catchier than *New York, Chicago & St. Louis Railroad Company; Cotton Belt* is easier to remember than *St. Louis Southwestern Railway Lines.*

Some older boxcars advertise the railroad's passenger trains ("Route of the *Vista Domes,*" "Route of the *Phoebe Snow*"), but these passenger trains are gone today, and the governments of the United States and Canada run all but a few of the long-distance trains that remain. Other boxcars mention the railroad's freight business. Old New York Central boxcars brag about that road's "Early Bird Service" and show a perky bird in a railroader's hat; the cars themselves were painted robin's-egg blue. Georgia's little Chattahoochee Dam Railroad amuses train watchers with its slogan "Better by a Dam Site."

A railroad's name usually tells something about where it runs. The Atchison, Topeka & Sante Fe connects those three cities. Illinois Central Gulf travels from Chicago, Illinois, to the Gulf of Mexico. Some names are more wishful than accurate. The Chicago, Rock Island & Pacific heads west from Chicago, passes through Rock Island, Iowa, but stops about a thousand miles short of salt water. The Philadelphia, Bethlehem & New England has a truly boastful name: this Pennsylvania line is but three miles long.

About half the cars you see nowadays bear the names of railroads which have been swallowed by bigger lines. Many boxcars carry the names of companies that no longer exist.

As a rule, the bigger the company, the less interesting the name. Whereas most railroad names are geographically inspired, the current trend among the huge merger railroads is to ignore place names and adopt a label that might describe almost any company. So it is that several eastern railroads were melted down into *Conrail;* the passenger services of dozens of lines, each with a colorful name and logo, were blended and renamed a grayish *Amtrak;* and half a dozen roads, including Seaboard Coast Line and Chesapeake & Ohio (with its mascot kittens, Chessie and Peake) have been corralled into the uninteresting but modern-sounding *CSX.*

Stenciled on each side of every car is its date of birth. *BLT 6 56* means the car was built in June of 1956. You'll notice that freight cars have far longer lives, on the average, than automobiles.

You may see the stenciled request that the car be sent home, when empty, to the freight agent at Shreveport, Louisiana, or Oneonta, New York, or another railroad town. A railroad company takes its cars only as far as the end of its line, as a rule, and then passes them on to another company. En route to its destination, a freight car may be handled by as many as four or five railroads.

At least as interesting as the railroad's official words and symbols are messages and doodles written on the sides in chalk. When a freight pulls into a yard, the conductor may walk down its length "chalking" on each car the railroad or industry to which it should be sent. People also like to doodle on cars, using them as huge billboards. One of the most commonly seen doodles is a cartoon of a man taking a siesta beneath a palm tree. The drawings are signed "Herby." Some forty thousand "Herby" doodles were riding around the country on freight cars before a St. Louis yard worker named Herbert took his retirement and admitted that he had been drawing Herby for decades.

Telephone box

Sign pinpoints location of bridge in miles (top number) and hundredths of a mile (bottom number)

$\dfrac{177}{51}$

Speed limit sign (top number for freights, bottom for passenger trains)

50

60

Handcar

Longer ties (with empty spike holes) show where another track branched off

READING THE RAILS

CHAPTER SIX

Railroads run fewer trains today than in the past. But even on a sleepy branch line with its weekly freight, a train watcher has much to look at.

That's because trains leave tracks—not just the steel ones they roll over, but the little marks and signs made in a century of traveling back and forth over the same piece of earth. You know how your personal clutter can build up in your room in just a day or two. Now consider that a railroad may have had a hundred and twenty-five years to build up what amounts to a museum of odds and ends. Stand at trackside and look around you. You'll see all sorts of clues as to what went on at the railroad, a century ago as well as just yesterday.

The railroad seems fond of placing little signs with numbers and letters on everything it owns, including stations, towers, bridges, and signals. Signs with just two letters are known as call signs, and they identify stations and towers. The signs are a carryover from the days when operators and station agents sent messages to one another by telegraph; the letters, HB or LT or MU, served as their addresses.

Mileposts tell railroaders how far they are from a city at one end of the line. The city's initial may be included with the number. Mileage signs of another sort are placed on trackside structures, tunnels, and bridges. Two numbers are used, one above the other in the manner of a fraction. The top one is the figure on the last milepost; the bottom one gives the distance from that post in hundredths of a mile. These signs enable a railroad to pinpoint just where these structures are, give or take a hundredth of a mile (just over 50 feet).

The railroad placed telephones wherever trains may have to make stops out on the line, such as at sidings, signals, and tunnels. The phones are usually old-fashioned, and housed in a little shelter known as a call box. To call a particular station agent or tower operator, a railroader has to give a certain number of twists on a crank that comes out of the phone. Now that many trains are equipped with radios, railroad call boxes aren't very common.

Another victim of changing technology is the water

tank. These were once stationed at intervals along every line to replenish the water supply of steam locomotive tenders. Small-town tanks were often made of cedar or cypress, woods that resisted rotting. More substantial tanks were of steel, brick, or stone. Of the thousands of tanks that once were common landmarks across the continent, few remain. Those brick and stone tanks left standing may remind you of the towers of ruined medieval castles.

If you look closely, you may spot little signs and numbers on ties and rails. Some railroads record the sharpness of curves with metal tags attached to ties. This figure is given in degrees and fractions of degrees, called minutes, in this fashion: 2′ 6″ means two degrees, six minutes. The sharpest curves approach eighteen degrees, and long cars may not be able to negotiate them without danger of derailing. Track workers refer to these numbers when adjusting a track to its proper alignment.

Railroads may also mark ties with the year that they were put down. A date nail, bearing the last two digits of the year, is driven into the top of the tie so that the railroad maintenance department can compare how long ties of various woods—oak, mulberry, locust, osage orange, sassafras—are holding up. Ties generally last about twenty years before decaying and splitting, but you may find some bearing date nails from the 1920s or even earlier.

Rails also will tell their age to those who know where

to look. Embossed on one side you'll find the name of the manufacturer, the year the rail was milled, and even the month as indicated by the number of parallel lines set in a row. It's not unusual to find rails in daily use that are half a century old.

A copper wire connecting each rail to the rails before and after it is a bond wire, an electrical link that shows the line is governed by automatic block signals.

While you're looking at ties, you might notice several in a row that get progressively longer on one side, for no apparent reason. If so, you have discovered an abandoned branch line or siding. These extended ties supported the first few yards of diverging track. The ties bear holes left by the spikes of the missing rails; often

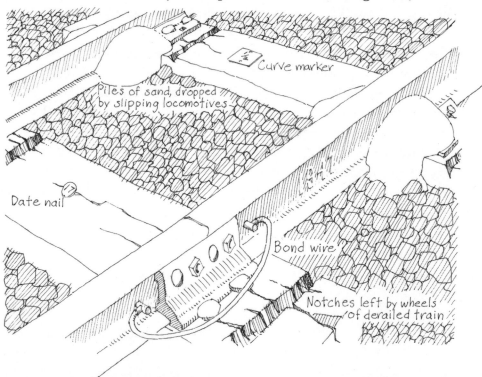

the holes are plugged with wooden pegs to keep the ties from rotting. If you look closely, you should be able to make out a path of cinders or gravel leading away from the tracks.

Where did that vanished track lead? To nothing more than a long-gone freight house or mill, perhaps, but possibly it could take you on a nice hike along a stream, past quarries and forgotten depots, over stone viaducts and wooden trestles, through tunnels, to villages all but vanished, and even to ghost towns.

Tracks may bear signs of trains in trouble. Miniature dunes of white sand, built up along the rails, tell that engineers had to drop sand from the locomotive's air-powered sanders to get better traction. These little dunes are found most often on hills, especially where a signal forces trains to come to a stop and start again. The rails may show shiny flat spots, too, where the big steel wheels have spun helplessly. If the tracks are too slippery with rain and oil, and sanding doesn't do the trick, then the crew of a heavy freight may split the string of cars in two and take one half up the hill at a time.

Trouble of a more serious sort is revealed by a series of notches in the ties, spaced as far apart as a train's wheels are from one another—not quite five feet. The notches were made by the wheels of derailed cars. Derailed cars may be dragged for miles before the crew notices something is amiss and can bring the train to a halt. (Cabooses have either bay windows or a cupola on top so that railroaders can look up the length of the train for problems like this.) Bridges are often equipped with a second set of rails to keep derailed cars from veering so far to one side that they'd plunge off the edge.

Finally, take a look at trackside litter. The wind blows discarded train orders, memos, and railroaders' lunch bags. You'll find dribbles of cargo, perhaps feed corn on its way to mills, some of it sprouting between the stones of the roadbed; and there may be purplish taconite pellets dropped on their way to a blast furnace to be melted into steel. You'll certainly come upon parts that fell off the tracks and the trains themselves—spikes, bolts, springs, brakes, and air hoses. Even whole locomotives have been left behind to astound the train watcher, ac-

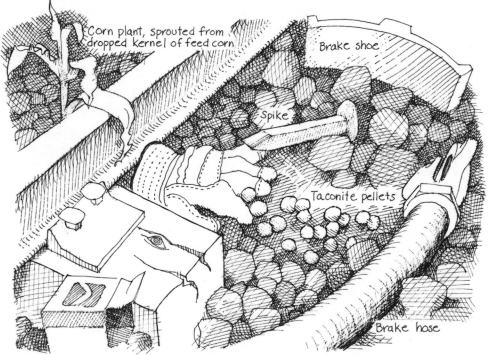

Corn plant, sprouted from dropped kernel of feed corn

Brake shoe

Spike

Taconite pellets

Brake hose

cording to local legends. More than one railroad town keeps alive the story of a steam engine that leaped from the tracks into a forest so deep and impenetrable that the railroad gave it up for lost.

The Long Life and Quick Death 🖎 of Norca, Pennsylvania

As you poke around the tracks for clues of what has gone on there, you are apt to pick up a painless lesson in local history. Almost any piece of track you happen upon will tell the stories of people, businesses, towns, and a way of life that flourished for a time and then faded away—leaving just enough of a trace to catch the attention of a train watcher with eyes and ears open. If you can make friends with a railroader, all the better.

I was happy to get to know Gene, a tower operator at Norca, in central Pennsylvania. I think Gene was happy to get to know me, too, because he must have been lonely. He had few trains to watch over on his night shift, and he rarely saw people because no highways passed through Norca. In fact, nobody lived there. This was a place so remote and unnoticed by the world that you couldn't find it on a map, unless it happened to be an especially good railroad map.

Norca had nothing but a tower, and it was a flimsy lit-

tle fiberboard tower at that. This shack hid on a wooded ledge tucked between the Susquehanna River and one of Pennsylvania's endless east-to-west mountains. The mountain kept Gene's tower in deep shade most of the day, and any light that did filter through was absorbed by tall trees and thickets of mountain laurel. It was a lovely place to watch trains. Streams fell off the mountainside, ducked under the tracks through stone bridges, and joined the wide, brown Susquehanna. Just outside Gene's door, a handsome old truss bridge carried a set of tracks across the river.

Norca came into existence because a tower was needed to govern train traffic where the tracks of one railroad crossed those of another. Such rail intersections are usually found in towns (or it might be more exact to say that where busy rail lines cross, a town will soon spring up). But Norca was perched on a bit of ground too narrow and dark for settlement.

Here is the region around Norca as it appeared at the turn of the century. Catawissa was a busy railroad hub, with two depots and its own opera house. Across the river, tiny Rupert was an important transportation center in spite of its size. Two railroads exchanged cars in a freight yard there. A big brick hotel offered lodging to passengers staying over for the night (some thirty passenger trains passed through the valley each day). On the still water of a canal, mule-drawn barges floated coal and grain toward the sea. A brick tower stood guard over

Norca. (Legend has it that *Norca* is an abbreviated form, or acronym, of *North Catawissa*.)

For nearly a hundred years, tower operators had guarded this intersection, through wars and national depressions, winter blizzards and spring rains that filled the Susquehanna until it lapped at the tracks. Gene liked to talk about the many operators who had served at Norca before him. He told the story of one man who had died on the job long ago. A freight train derailed and toppled the brick tower into the Susquehanna. Gene pointed out where bricks and bits of concrete could still be found under the leaves and bushes.

This story revealed why Gene always left his little tower when a train approached. Certainly the job didn't call for him to do so. He just wanted to have a head start up the mountainside in case history should repeat itself and a train jump the rails. He showed me a clear area behind the shack. "My escape trail," he explained. "A big freight hits the ground and I'm up that mountain like a shot."

By about 1970, one of the lines out of Catawissa was gone and the depots had been closed. A small switch engine was stored here, and each morning it crossed the river to move cars about the Rupert yard, but Catawissa was no longer much of a railroad town. In these parts, the town was better known for the Catawissa Bottling Works, makers of sky-blue Big Ben's Birch Beer and tiny brown bottles of a ginger beer so peppery you couldn't drink it with your eyes open. The canal was just a shallow ditch full of frogs and tin cans. The Rupert hotel stood empty, with its windows knocked out; on one side, dim block letters still advertised HOTEL. For many years, the Iron City Express traveled through the valley on its overnight trip between Scranton and Pittsburgh, offering sleeping accommodations and a dining car, but by this time passenger trains had been discontinued. In his fiberboard tower, Gene the operator declared sadly, "The railroad has gone to the dogs." He said the railroad was not well. And he was in a position to know, having taken the pulse of the two lines simply by noticing that fewer and fewer trains passed each year. Traffic was too light, he said. Both lines were sick.

Not long after he made his diagnosis, one of the two railroads discontinued service past the tower and its track was ripped up. The intersection was no more. And Norca, because it was nothing but a railroad address, ceased to be.

The little tower was torn down. Gene retired to his big white house in a village a ways up the abandoned line. A few years later, the second line was taken out, and Catawissa was without any of the railroads that had nourished it into a good-sized town. In Rupert, the old brick hotel was leveled, but a single rail line remained. Once a week or so, there was a rumble along the quiet Susquehanna Valley as a slow freight rolled over this last set of tracks.

Today, Norca is marked only by two flat roadbeds that cross in the woods. The spot now looks more like it did a thousand years ago than just a few years back. Nature is quick to heal the scratches made across the earth by railroads. Before long, leaves will sift over the gravel roadbeds, trees will reclaim the space where trains once sped, and a mystery will have been sown for future generations of train watchers. What caused the remarkably flat paths through the laurel thickets? And those bricks under the forest litter; why would anyone have wanted to put a building in this forgotten place?

ROGER YEPSEN grew up near Schenectady, N.Y., and has vivid memories of overnight trips on the New York Central to visit his grandparents in Indiana. After teaching art to third through twelfth graders at a central school in New York State, he played in a rock band for a while, then went on to work in a government flood relief program. Currently an editor in the book division of Rodale Press, Mr. Yepsen lives in Bethlehem, Pa., with his wife and their two children. He goes train watching almost every day.